DISCOVER ANCIENT CIVILIZATIONS

# DISCOVER ANCIENT PERSIA

Neil D. Bramwell

**Enslow Publishers, Inc.**
40 Industrial Road
Box 398
Berkeley Heights, NJ 07922
USA
http://www.enslow.com

At its peak, Darius' empire stretched over three continents.

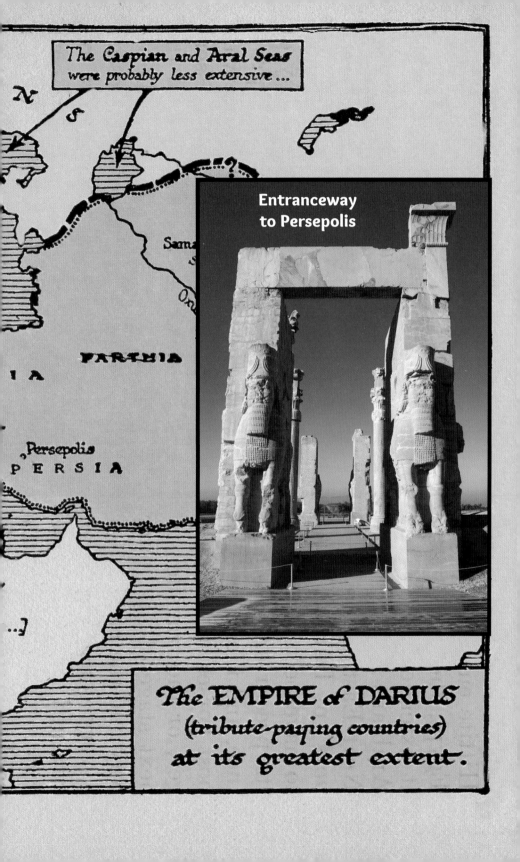

The Caspian and Aral Seas were probably less extensive...

N

PARTHIA

Sama

On

Persepolis
PERSIA

Entranceway to Persepolis

The EMPIRE of DARIUS (tribute-paying countries) at its greatest extent.

Original edition published as *Ancient Persia* © 2004 by Enslow Publishers, Inc.

**Library of Congress Cataloging-in-Publication Data**:
Bramwell, Neil D., 1932-
  Discover ancient Persia / Neil D. Bramwell.
     p. cm. — (Discover ancient civilizations)
  Summary: "Learn about the art and cultural contributions, family life, religions and people of ancient Persia"—Provided by publisher.
  Includes bibliographical references and index.
  ISBN 978-0-7660-4198-1
  1. Iran—Civilization—To 640—Juvenile literature.  I. Title.
  DS267.B73 2014
  935.7—dc23
                              2012011574

**Future editions:**
Paperback ISBN: 978-1-4644-0339-2          Single-User PDF ISBN: 978-1-4646-1189-6
ePUB ISBN: 978-1-4645-1189-9               Multi-User PDF: 978-0-7660-5818-7

Printed in the United States of America
112013 Lake Book Manufacturing, Inc., Melrose Park, IL
10 9 8 7 6 5 4 3 2 1

**To Our Readers:** We have done our best to make sure all Internet Addresses in this book were active and appropriate when we went to press. However, the author and the publisher have no control over and assume no liability for the material available on those Internet sites or on other Web sites they may link to. Comments can be sent to comments@enslow.com or to the address on the back cover.

♻ Enslow Publishers, Inc., is committed to printing our books on recycled paper. The paper in every book contains 10% to 30% post-consumer waste (PCW). The cover board on the outside of each book contains 100% PCW. Our goal is to do our part to help young people and the environment too!

**Photo Credits::** © 2012 Photos.com, a division of Getty Images. All rights reserved., pp. 44-45, 60, 64-65, 70-71, 78-79, 89; Aliraza Khatri/©2012 Photos.com, a division of Getty Images. All rights reserved., pp. 18-19;AP Photo/Vahid Salemi, p. 13; Clipart/©2012 Photos.com, a division of Getty Images. All rights reserved., pp. 2 -3, 9, 14(inset), 21, 22, 30, 35, 36, 51, 56, 61, 87(inset); Feodor Vasilevich Korolevsky /© 2012 Photos.com, a division of Getty Images. All rights reserved., p. 41; From *Wonders of the Past* , ©G.P. Putnam's Sons, 1923, p. 47; Hemera/©2013 Thinkstock, a division of Getty Images, pp. 84-85; iStock/©2013 Thinkstock, a division of Getty Images, pp. 75, 87; Nancy Nehring/ ©2012 Photos.com, a division of Getty Images. All rights reserved., p. 59; Shutterstock. com, pp. 2-3(Inset), 32-33, 90-91; Stefan Baum /©2012 Photos.com, a division of Getty Images. All rights reserved.,p. 48;Valery Shanin /©2012 Photos.com, a division of Getty Images. All rights reserved., pp. 26-27;Wikipedia Public domain image, pp. 14, 67, 68, 80.

**Cover Credits**:  Persepolis gateway: Shutterstock.com; Gold plaque with male figure (Inset): ©2012 Photos.com, a division of Getty Images. All rights reserved.

# Table of CONTENTS

CHAPTER 1  **The Empire of Cyrus the Great** .................... 7

CHAPTER 2  **The Land and Early History of Ancient Persia** ...................... 16

CHAPTER 3  **The Rise of the Hellenic League** .......................... 40

CHAPTER 4  **Language, Religion, and People** .................................. 53

CHAPTER 5  **Arts and Cultural Contributions** ............................ 73

CHAPTER 6  **The Government of Ancient Persia** ........................... 82

**Timeline** ................................................94

**Glossary** ...............................................95

**Chapter Notes** ......................................97

**Further Reading** ................................101

**Internet Addresses** ...........................102

**Index** ..................................................103

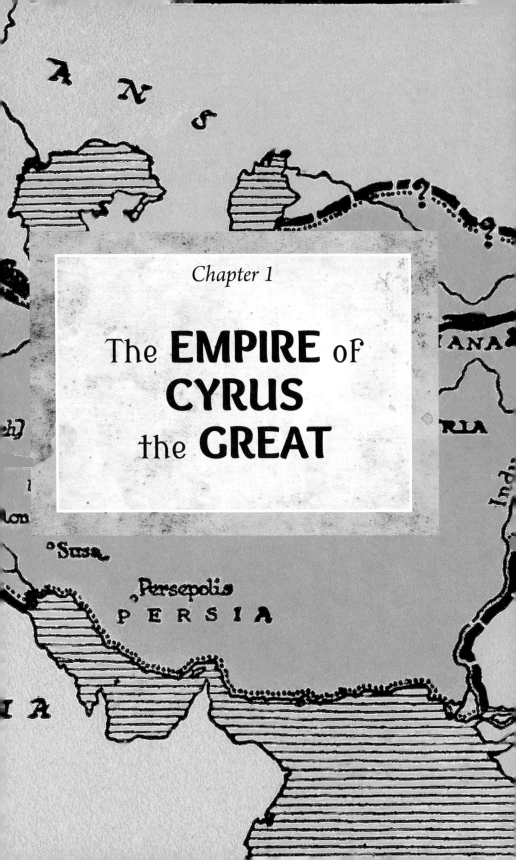

Chapter 1

# The **EMPIRE** of **CYRUS** the **GREAT**

In the sixth century B.C., the land that is today the nation of Iran was the center of the largest empire in the ancient world. The kings of Ancient Persia (from Persis, the Greeks' name for Persia) were the leaders of a great civilization that made important advances in government, laws, and communications. The Persian Empire founded by Cyrus the Great in 550 B.C. would, within only fifty years, occupy much of the known world at the time.

## The Aryans and Medes

The earliest people in what is now Iran were the Elamites, who may have settled the region as early as 3000 B.C. Aryans, nomadic people from central Asia, began migrating to Iran in the 1500s B.C. After a time, there were two major groups of Aryans: the Medes in the northwest, who established a kingdom called Media, and the Persians in southern Iran. Both of

**Cyrus the Great**

these groups referred to their home as Iran, which translates as "land of the Aryans." By the 600s B.C. the Medes ruled the Persians. But the rule of the Medes came to an end between 559 B.C. and 549 B.C., when a Persian who would come to be known as Cyrus the Great overthrew Astyages, king of the Medes. He is the first ruler to whose name was added the words the Great, a title taken by many others after him, including Alexander the Great, who over-threw the Achaemenid dynasty two centuries after the death of Cyrus.

## The Achaemenid Empire of Cyrus the Great

According to Herodotus, a Greek historian, Cyrus was the son of an Iranian nobleman and a Median princess, daughter of the Median king Astyages. Many historians dispute this account of Cyrus' background, but what cannot be disputed is that his dynasty, the Achaemenids, would rule the vast Persian Empire for more than two hundred fifty years.

Cyrus began to build his empire after the model of the great Assyrian Empire that had flourished centuries before on the banks of the Tigris River, in what is now the country of Iraq. By 545 B.C., Cyrus had seized the kingdom of Lydia, and he gradually took over the Greek colonies in Ionia, in western Asia Minor, a peninsula in western Asia between the Black Sea and the Mediterranean Sea that is now the Asian part of Turkey. By 539 B.C., Cyrus' armies had conquered Babylonia, and Cyrus freed the Jews who were in captivity there, allowing them to return to Palestine, which was also under his control. Although he did not conquer Egypt, he prepared the way for his son, Cambyses II, to accomplish that, in 525 B.C.

## A Benevolent Ruler

Cyrus' rule came to an end in 530 B.C. with his death. The empire he began would not reach its peak until the reign of Darius I, in 500 B.C., when it would encompass a region nearly as large as the modern continental United States. But Cyrus the Great continues to be admired among ancient world leaders for more than his military conquests and the empire he began.

What set Cyrus the Great apart from the rulers of most other ancient dynasties was his attitude toward the different ethnic and religious groups that existed within his empire. He had conquered many lands, and the people within those lands spoke different languages, prayed to different gods, and lived according to different customs. His tolerance and respect for the diverse cultures, customs, and beliefs of his people

The Cyrus Cylinder is displayed at the
National Museum of Iran, in Tehran,
September 12, 2010. The Cylinder is a
sixth century B.C. clay object inscribed with
an account in cuneiform of the conquest
of Babylon by the Persian King Cyrus the
Great and his intention to rule the
conquered people with fairness.

This bas-relief can be seen found at Pasargadae, northeast of Persepolis. A winged-figure thought to be Cyrus the Great is shown with four Assyrian wings, and wearing a horned Egyptian-like crown and Persian dress. At the top, the inscription written in three languages is the sentence "I am Cyrus the king, an Achaemenian." It reflects Cyrus's dedication to the philosophy of multiculturalism.

has led most historians to consider Cyrus a liberator rather than a conqueror.

Cyrus is also credited with being the author of what is often referred to as the first charter of human rights. The Cyrus Cylinder is an account of Cyrus' Babylonian conquest, written in cuneiform inscription on a clay cylinder. But it is remarkable for its declarations of reform. In the ancient script, Cyrus pledges to bring relief to Babylon's citizens and return captives held prisoner in Babylon to their homelands:

"I returned to the sacred cities . . . the sanctuaries of which have been in ruins for a long time, the images which used to live therein and established for them permanent sanctuaries. I gathered all their (former) inhabitants and returned (to them) their habitations."[1]

Chapter 2

# The LAND and EARLY HISTORY of ANCIENT PERSIA

By 490 B.C. the Persian Empire was the largest empire that the ancient world had ever known. The Persian king, Darius I, ruled over an area that stretched east to west from the Indus River in Pakistan to Asia Minor, including Thrace, an ancient country that is now part of Bulgaria and Turkey.

The empire from north to south extended from the Caspian Sea and the Black Sea down to the Arabian Sea, the Persian Gulf, and the Red Sea. What are now parts of Pakistan, Afghanistan, Iran, Turkey, Iraq, Syria, and Egypt were all once part of the great Persian Empire.

This vast territory encompassed great desert areas, mountain ranges, rugged seacoasts, and large fertile plains and valleys. The home area of the Persians was Persis, now called Fars, in southwestern Iran's Zagros Mountains. The wide variety of terrain included the deserts of Egypt, fertile and green only along either side of the Nile,

A view of the Indus River in Pakistan. The Persian king, Darius I, ruled over an area that stretched east to west from the Indus River in Pakistan to Asia Minor.

to the mountainous terrain of Afghanistan. Large areas of the empire were desert or land so dry that crops could be grown only with large irrigation systems, which the Persians maintained throughout the empire. An inscription found in Egypt begun by Darius I and completed by Darius II describes underground channels dug for the flow of water.[1]

Early reference in history to the Persians as a distinct people occurs in the records of the Assyrian Empire of the ninth to seventh centuries B.C.[2] The Assyrian records refer to the Persians and the Medes. The Medes, who occupied a territory to the north of the Persians, were united and strong enough to defeat, with the aid of the Babylonians, the Assyrian Empire in 608 B.C.[3]

The Persians had formed a small kingdom in the region of modern-day Fars in Iran. The kingdom's first king, Teispes, is

King Darius I followed by attendants.

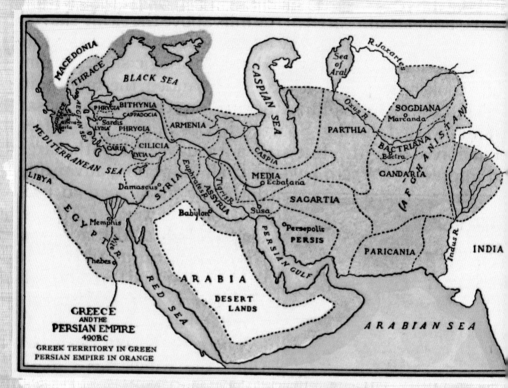

**Greece and Persia in 490 B.C.**

described on the Cyrus Cylinder as king and ancestor of Cyrus the Great.[4] However, according to an inscription ordered by Darius I, the founder of the Achaemenid dynasty was Achaemenes, father of Teispes.[5]

## Cyrus the Great

Cyrus II, also known as "Cyrus the Great," began the Persian Empire with the conquest of the Medes' homeland, Media, in 550 B.C. Within thirty years, Cyrus had completed Persia's conquest of all the countries that would make up the Persian Empire with the exception of Egypt. Cyrus' conquest of the Medes brought Persia to the borders of Lydia on the west coast of Asia Minor. Croesus, reputed to be the richest man in the world, was Lydia's king.

Croesus invaded Persia and was defeated by Cyrus in the Lydian capital of Sardis. In 546 B.C., Croesus was taken captive, and Lydia became part of the

Persian Empire.[6] Persia's conquest of Lydia was significant since it brought under Persian domination all the Ionian cities previously controlled by Lydia. The Greek city-states of Athens and Eretria then came to the aid of the Ionians, which led to the Persian wars against the mainland Greeks.

Persia now confronted the powerful Babylonian Empire, which stretched from the borders of Egypt to the borders of Persia at the Zagros Mountains. Babylonia's king, Nabonidus, was already under attack at home when Cyrus invaded Babylonia and took Nabonidus prisoner in 539 B.C. Cyrus freed the Jews who had been held in captivity in Babylon and helped them to establish a homeland in Palestine. His reign was characterized by a tolerance for the diverse people, languages, and religious beliefs that existed in the corners of his vast empire.

## Death of Cyrus the Great and Succession of Cambyses

Before his death, Cyrus had extended his lands from the Aegean Sea in the west to the Indus River and what is today Pakistan in the far east. Cyrus had also established a system of satrapies, or provinces, in the empire that were administered by satraps, or governors. In 529 B.C., Cyrus died in battle in the northeast of the empire near the Jaxartes River.[7]

Following Cyrus' death, Cambyses II succeeded his father as the leader of the Persian Empire. Cyrus named Cambyses as his successor, and prior to his death, Cyrus shared his rule with Cambyses.[8]

Cyrus' conquest of Babylonia had brought Persia to the borders of Egypt. Cambyses prepared to complete the conquest by first building a Persian Navy and taking control of the island of Cyprus

Persepolis was burned by Alexander the Great in 331 B.C. Only the columns, stairways, and door jambs of its great palaces survived the fire. The stairways, adorned with reliefs representing the king, his court, and delegates of his empire bringing gifts, demonstrate the might of the Persian monarch.

from the Egyptians.[9] In 525 B.C., Cambyses invaded Egypt and defeated the Egyptian pharaoh and his army at Memphis. With this victory, the once great empire of Egypt became part of the Persian Empire, ruled by Cambyses.

## Death of Cambyses and Succession of Darius I

Cambyses died in 522 B.C. on his way back to Persia to put down a rebellion led by a member of the Persian court. The leader of the rebellion was himself murdered by seven Persian nobles. One of those nobles, Darius I, then became king of the Persians in 522 B.C.[10]

As soon as Darius became king, however, rebellions against his rule broke out throughout the empire, and Darius spent a year putting them down. Once he had established control over all of the Persian Empire, he marked that control by having a large memorial carved onto the face of a cliff in a mountain peak at Behistun. Now known as the Behistun Inscription, the memorial proclaimed Darius' right to the throne and his success in putting down the rebellions. The inscriptions are inscribed in Elamite, Akkadian, and the new Old Persian script that Darius ordered created especially for the memorial. The inscriptions were copied into local languages and sent throughout the empire.[11]

## The Persian Wars Against the Greeks

Darius then completed the conquest of northwestern India, extending the Persian Empire to the east. He set about to establish a foothold in Europe by crossing the Dardanelles, a narrow strait that separates Asia Minor from Europe and connects the Aegean Sea with the Sea of Marmara. Darius' armies conquered Thrace, an ancient country on the Balkan Peninsula that had

The site at Behistun features this bas-relief and cuneiform inscription on a cliff 100 meters above ground level. It shows Darius holding a bow, as a sign of sovereignty, and treading on the chest of a figure that lies on his back before him. Darius faces nine rebel chiefs whose hands are bound behind them.

been ruled by Greece. He was also able to forge an alliance with the king of Macedonia, an ancient kingdom north of Greece.

The stage was now set for Darius to attack the Greek mainland in the first of what would become known as the Persian Wars. In 490 B.C., a larger Persian force attacked a smaller Athenian army at Marathon, a site north of Athens, but was defeated. The Persians lost 6,400 men to the Athenians' 192.[12] Darius retreated back to Persia, still in control of Thrace and the Ionian cities.

Darius died in 486 B.C., having expanded the Persian Empire into southeastern Europe and what is now southern Pakistan. He proved himself to be the true successor to Cyrus the Great by continuing to restore the Jewish state and seeing that the Temple was rebuilt in Jerusalem in 515. Darius also expanded upon Cyrus' system

The tomb of Cyrus the Great stands in Pasargadae, once a capital of the Persian Empire.

of satrapies, developed a system of taxation organized a new uniform monetary system. The great palaces at Persepolis and Susa, which were two of his capitals, were built during his reign. Finally, Darius established the absolute power of the Persian monarch, known as the King of Kings.

## Xerxes' Revenge and Defeats

Upon Darius' death in 486 B.C., he was succeeded by his son, Xerxes, who began his reign by putting down rebellions in Egypt and Babylonia. Xerxes then set about avenging his father's defeat at Marathon by launching an attack on the Greek mainland. Xerxes' aim was not only to avenge the defeat at Marathon but also to establish Persian control over the Aegean Sea and the eastern Mediterranean Sea.

In 481, Xerxes assembled an army estimated at two hundred thousand men from all over the Persian Empire.[13] The army was

The Greeks were facing invasion by Darius of Persia, whose warships landed in the Bay of Marathon. Despite being heavily outnumbered the Greeks surrounded the enemy troops and drove them back to the sea, losing only 192 men, while 6,000 Persians perished.

Xeres saw his forces destroyed at Salamis. More than eight hundred Persian ships were rammed and shattered by the Greeks.

supported by a naval fleet of one thousand ships, and both gathered at the Dardanelles to cross from Asia Minor into Europe. The powerful Greek city-states of Athens and Sparta, longtime rivals, combined their forces to fight the Persian invasion. At Thermopylae, a narrow mountain pass that led to central Greece, the Persians forced the Greeks to retreat, although a small Spartan force led by the Spartan king, Leonidas, fought bravely and delayed the Persian advance. The Persian Army then moved into Athens, which offered no resistance since its citizens had evacuated to nearby islands, and the Persians burned the city.

But after Xerxes' naval forces were defeated by the Greeks at Salamis and Plataea, Persia made no more attempts to invade mainland Greece. Instead, Persia attempted to weaken the Greek city-states by bribing their leaders and assisting individual Greek states in their wars against each other. Xerxes' reign came to an end in 465 B.C. when he and his heir were murdered.

## Later Achaemenid Rulers

Artaxerxes I, who next ruled Persia, may have been involved in the murder.[14]

Artaxerxes I was succeeded briefly by Xerxes II and then in 423 B.C. by his son, who took the name Darius II. After becoming king, Darius II waged war for several months against two of his brothers who tried to overthrow him. Throughout his reign, Darius II was engaged in putting down rebellions. In 404 B.C., Darius sent aid to the Spartans to assist them in their war against Athens.[15]

Darius II was succeeded by his son, Artaxerxes II, in 404 B.C. Artaxerxes II then had to battle his younger brother, Cyrus, who claimed the throne. Cyrus and the ten thousand Greek soldiers he paid to fight for him were finally defeated in battle by Artaxerxes II in 401 B.C. Artaxerxes II's reign was notable in reestablishing Persian rule over Egypt in 387 B.C., and he again put the Ionian cities under Persian control. It was also the longest reign, forty-six years, of any Persian king. He died in 359 B.C.

For the next twenty-three years, the Persian Empire was again plunged into rebellion, with rightful heirs to the throne being murdered. In 336, a member of another branch of the Achaemenid family was made the ruler of Persia. Named Codomannus at birth, he took the name Darius III. Darius III would be the last Achaemenid king of the Persian Empire.

Chapter 3

# The RISE of the HELLENIC LEAGUE

After Philip, king of Macedonia, had established Macedonia's domination over all of the city-states of mainland Greece, he called for an invasion of the Persian Empire. He forced the formation of the Greek city-states into the Hellenic League (Hellas being the Greek name for "Greece") by proclaiming himself and his descendants its leader. The Hellenic League, with Philip in charge, then approved the invasion of the Persian Empire.[1]

In 336 B.C., Philip sent a force across the Dardanelles to seize a foothold in Asia Minor for the invasion of Persia. Darius III was unable to force the Greek Army back across the Dardanelles, and they remained there until Philip's son, Alexander, began his invasion of Persia.[2]

**A gold coin depicting Alexander the Great.**

## Alexander the Great Begins His Conquests

Philip was murdered in 336 B.C., and his son, Alexander, who would become known as "Alexander the Great " for his military victories, succeeded to the throne of Macedonia. Alexander had to first put down rebellions by the Greek city-states, but after that had been done, in 335 B.C., he began his conquest of Persia. At the river Granicus in Asia Minor, Alexander met and defeated a huge Persian Army led by Darius III's son-in-law, Mithridates, who was killed in the battle.[3]

## Darius' Defeat at Issus

After the victory at Granicus, Alexander continued his march into Persia. Persian cities including Sardis and Ephesus were soon in Alexander's control, and he conquered Miletus, a seaport in western Asia Minor. Darius III had done little to stop Alexander's advance. Darius moved first to Susa and then to Babylon where he made the decision to lead his army against the Macedonian king.

The two armies met at Issus (which is now part of Syria) in 333 B.C. The battle was a disastrous defeat for Darius III who fled the leaving behind the royal family and great treasure. Darius fled so far so fast, that Alexander was able to capture Darius' family as prisoners in the process. Darius offered Alexander ransom for the royal family as well as promising territory, but Alexander refused.[4]

## Alexander's Conquest of Egypt

Alexander continued his conquests by marching down the coast of Asia, conquering and subduing the Persian possessions there, including a seven-month siege at Tyre. Finally he reached Egypt and conquered it in 332 B.C.[5]

This mosaic shows Alexander leading his army against Darius II's Persian forces at the Battle of Issus. As his charioteer tries to drive the royal chariot away, Darius, in the center, looks back anxiously toward the advancing Alexander.

## Gaugamela: Destruction of the Persian Army

In 331 B.C., Alexander marched his troops to Gaugamela, near the Tigris River in what is today Syria. There he met the Persian Army led by Darius. Alexander's forces destroyed Darius' Persian Army and Darius fled, leaving the royal treasure behind in the Persian capitals.[6] Babylon and Susa surrendered to Alexander, who marched on to Persepolis, a magnificent Persian capital whose palaces had been built by Darius I. Alexander looted and burned the city to the ground in revenge for Xerxes' destruction of the temples at Athens.[7]

## End of the Achaemenid Empire: Death of Darius

Alexander continued his pursuit of Darius and his forces into the northeastern parts of the Persian Empire, but one of Darius' generals, Bessos, stabbed Darius to death in

330 B.C., as Alexander was about to catch up with them.[8] Alexander pursued Bessos, who had declared himself king of Persia, caught him, and took him prisoner. Bessos was tortured, then executed in 329 B.C. as the assassin of Darius III.[9]

With Darius III's death the Persian Empire under the Achaemenid dynasty came to an end. Alexander would rule the Persians until his empire ended with his death in 323 in Babylon. At that time Alexander's generals carved up his empire into several kingdoms, with Ptolemy I taking Egypt. Ptolemy's dynasty ruled Egypt until it became part of the Roman Empire in 30 B.C.

## Later Persian Empires

Seleucus, who had been one of Alexander's generals, began a dynasty known as the Seleucid dynasty more than ten years after Alexander's death. The Seleucids ruled

These two great piers, standing about 11 yards high and carved in deep relief with two bulls in the Assyrian manner symbolizing power are remains of the monumental entrance built by Xerxes on the Platform of Palaces at Persepolis.

An imagined view of
the Platform of Palaces
at Persepolis.

Persia and nearby regions and were responsible for founding many cities and introducing Greek culture into parts of western and central Asia. In about 250 B.C., a group known as the Parthians took control of Persia and created an empire that lasted until about A.D. 224. Their rulers were engaged in fighting Rome in the west and the Kushans in the east, in what is now Afghanistan, as well as putting down civil wars within their empire. In 224, what was left of the Persian Empire was once again controlled by a Persian, Ardashir, who overthrew the Parthians and established the Sassanid dynasty, named for Ardashir's grandfather, Sassan. The dynasty founded by Ardashir would rule for four centuries, until it was overthrown in 651 The Persians continued their wars with Rome, scoring several significant victories in the mid-500s and recapturing lands that had once belonged to Persia during the Achaemenid Empire. But

Alexander kneels beside the body of Darius III.
Darius's death also marked the end of the
Persian Empire under the Achaemenid Empire.

the defeats at Constantinople, then the capital of the Byzantine Empire, made them withdraw from the lands they had conquered. With the rise of Islam in the 600s, a new religion begun in Arabia, the Sassanid dynasty came to an end.

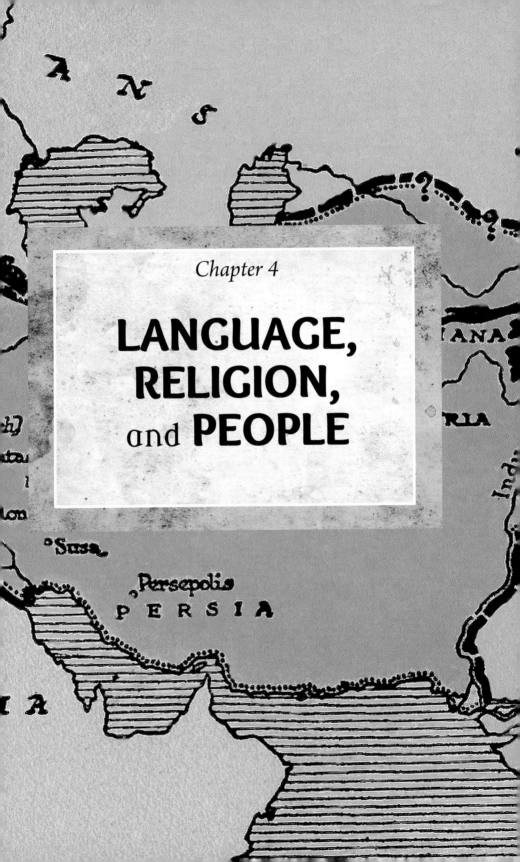

Chapter 4

# LANGUAGE, RELIGION, and PEOPLE

The Persian kings were tolerant of the individual cultures of the countries they had conquered: They allowed the customs and languages of the conquered peoples, including those of the Egyptians, Greeks, and Babylonians, to continue.

The Persians spoke an Indo-European language known as Old Persian, which was the official language of the empire. But Aramaic, a Semitic language related to Hebrew that had long been in use in the various countries conquered by the Persians, was the most widely used language in the Persian Empire. There is no Old Persian script that has been found to exist until after the conquests. In addition to Greek writers such as Herodotus and Xenophon, Babylonian sources, and the Old Testament, a major source of our knowledge of Persia comes from royal inscriptions and official archives of the empire. Particularly important are inscriptions carved on giant memorials that offer detailed accounts of the conquests of the kings. At times the inscriptions on the monuments are carved in three languages: Elamite, the language of the earliest people in Persia; Akkadian, the language of the Babylonians; and Persian.

## Respect for Religious Beliefs

The Persian kings' attitude toward religion was also marked by respect and even active support of the religions of each conquered country.[1] The cuneiform inscriptions on the Cyrus Cylinder record how Cyrus the Great restored the ruined sanctuaries in Babylonia after his conquest of Babylon. Perhaps the most famous indication of the Cyrus's respect for religion comes from a passage in the Old Testament of the Christian Bible. It praises Cyrus the Great for permitting the Jews who had been exiled to Babylon to return to Jerusalem with instructions to rebuild their temple.[2]

Cyrus the Great restores the vessels of the temple to the Hebrew exiles. Cyrus liberated the Hebrew exiles to resettle and rebuild Jerusalem and to reconstruct their temple, earning him an honored place in Judaism.

An inscription in Egypt records that Cyrus'
son, Cambyses, restored Egyptian temples
and worshiped in accordance with the
Egyptian rites after his conquest of Egypt.[3]

## Early Worship

Before the reign of Cyrus the Great, many
people in Persia worshiped local gods or
spirits associated with agriculture, war, and
the important aspects of everyday life.
Animals, ancestors, and the stars were all
objects of worship. Worship was marked by
animal sacrifice and the use of fire in the
religious rites. There was no organized
priesthood or religious doctrine, but learned
men known as magi sometimes assisted in
carrying out religious rites.[4]

## Zoroastrianism and the Persians

Zoroaster was a prophet who founded a
religion, Zoroastrianism, that had a great
influence upon the Persian rulers of the
Achaemenid dynasty. Zoroaster's exact

lifetime is not known, but evidence suggests it was before Achaemenid rule.[5] Zoroaster adapted some of the older beliefs with new ideas and combined these into a unified system of belief. Zoroastrian beliefs were handed down orally throughout the Achaemenid period. A written text of Zoroastrian beliefs was compiled in the fourth century A.D.[6]

## The Duality of Good vs. Evil

The doctrine of Zoroastrianism that existed in the Achaemenid period was based on Zoroaster's teachings that the universe was comprised of good and evil spirits constantly at war with one another. Zoroaster taught that Ahura Mazda headed the good spirits as the supreme god, representing good, light, and truth. Opposed to him were the evil spirits led by a god of darkness, Ahriman. The two gods struggled for control of the universe with men and women in the

Darius I claimed credit for inventing the Old Persian cuneiform script, pictured, but most scholars think that Darius commissioned his scribes to come up with this early form of writing.

**Carved Representation of Ahura Mazda At Persepolis.**

According to the great teacher Zoroaster, the world is a stage for unceasing conflict between the powers of Light and Darkness, or Good and Evil.

..............................

middle. The most significant features of Zoroastrianism were its belief in a supreme god and the idea that humans were free to choose between good and evil. It also taught that humans will be judged at their death, with good deeds rewarded and evil deeds punished.[7]

## Zoroastrian Worship

Zoroastrian worship took place in temples and out of doors at altars, with fire playing an important part in purification rituals. Fire, together with water and earth, were revered as the natural manifestations of

Ahura Mazda and were regarded as sacred. In early Zoroastrianism, magi assisted in the religious rites. Later Zoroastrian priests exercised a great influence over the government of the Achaemenid rulers, and for a time, Zoroastrianism became the state religion, although other religions continued to flourish.

As long as they accepted Persian rule, the people living in the Persian Empire during the Achaemenid period, who were from many different ethnic groups, were allowed to live according to their own cultures, religion, and traditional practices.

## Families

Early in the Persian Empire, as with many ancient cultures, families were formed into clans, and clans were part of larger groups known as tribes. But with the growth of the empire, these large family units began to disappear.

Most Persian men had more than one wife, and large families were encouraged. The king even rewarded families with the most children.[8] Persian society was dominated by men, from the government led by the king to the husband in charge of the family. Men's dominance in Persian society is evident by the fact that no women appear in any of the surviving monumental reliefs of the kings and his court and subject peoples. Women also apparently began to wear veils during the reign of Cyrus the Great.[9]

Women, did, however, own and manage property, and they traveled to the far reaches of the empire when necessary to manage it. Tablets at Persepolis record how Artystone, wife of Darius I, traveled to her various estates, receiving provisions on the journey. Artystone had her own seal, which she used to sign receipts for provisions issued to her on her journeys.[10]

Courtiers depicted on the stairway to the Royal Audience Hall of Darius I at Persepolis.

Persian clothing mainly consisted of caftans, or long robes, with jewelry as an important part of their attire. While the nobility lived in palaces and stone houses, most commoners lived in mud huts.

## Farmers and Artisans

Persians who were not part of the ruling class were mostly farmers. In different parts of the empire, farmers grew corn, grain, barley, sesame seed for oil, cotton, and flax. Dates were another important crop that at times they were used as money to pay debts. Cattle, sheep, and goats were raised throughout the empire.

Artisans were important to the ruling classes of the empire. The Persian kings employed large numbers of skilled artisans from many different regions. The great complex at Susa built by Darius I contains inscriptions that list artisans and materials from all over the empire that were used in

**King (second, left) with courtiers**

**King in battle dress (center) with soldiers**

Susa's construction. Timber from Lebanon, gold from Sardis, lapis lazuli and carnelian from Uzbekistan, ebony from Egypt, and ivory from India are among the materials and sources described. Men, women, and children from every part of the empire, including Ionia, Sardis, Babylon, Egypt, and India, were employed in the king's service as stone workers, coppersmiths, beer tenders, wine makers, and weavers.[11]

## Education

There were no formal schools for the Persians living during the Achaemenid period, and only the sons of the nobility received tutoring. At the age of five, a son was removed from his mother's care to be taught the value of truth. Throughout Persian culture, it was considered disgraceful to lie. The sons of the common people were trained in horseback riding, hunting with bow and arrow, and the

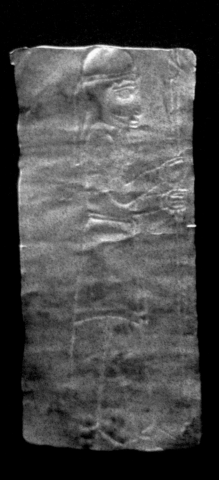

Rectangular Plaques, Achaemenid Persian (5th–4th Century B.C.). Wrought of thin delicate gold, five male figures wearing belted tunics are represented on these diminutive plaques. Many of these warriors hold spears in a formal and upright stance. Their solid erect posture is reminiscent of the high-relief figures on the façade of the Audience Hall at Persepolis.

throwing of a spear, much as their nomadic ancestors had been.[12] Although some women had been known to have reached statesman level importance, formal education was restricted to boys.

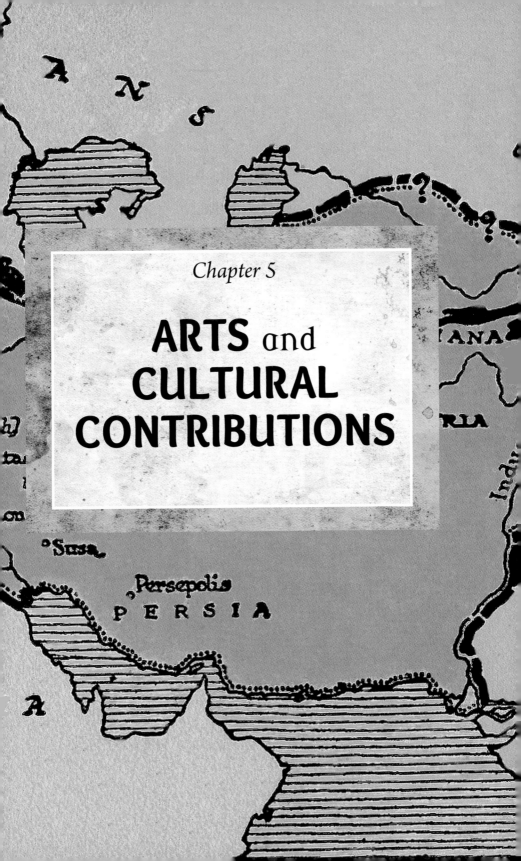

Chapter 5

# ARTS and CULTURAL CONTRIBUTIONS

The art of Persia was a product of the influences of the art of the conquered peoples who lived in the empire. Elements of Greek, Egyptian, and Assyrian art were taken by the Persian kings and mixed and reworked to produce an art that then became Persian.[1] The ruins of the capital at Pasargadae built by Cyrus the Great and at the great complexes built at Susa and Persepolis by Darius I show the influences of many cultures.

## Pasargadae

Cyrus the Great built his royal capital at Pasargadae with a number of palaces surrounded by lush gardens. The buildings featured huge columned halls decorated with monumental reliefs. Workmen from all over the empire (some who were prisoners of war) were employed in the construction of these palaces.[2] Pasargadae was the place where ceremonies marking the

**The ruins of one of the palaces at Pasargadae**

king's succession to the throne were held. It was also Cyrus's last resting place and is today an archaeological site and one of Iran's UNESCO World Heritage Sites.

## Persepolis

Persepolis is the Greek name (from perses polis for "Persian City") for the ancient city of Parsa, located seventy miles northeast of Shiraz in present-day Iran. The name Parsa meant "City of The Persians". Darius I began the construction of the palace complex at Persepolis, and it was continued by Xerxes and Artaxerxes I. The city of Persepolis, built atop an artificial stone terrace, covered an area of about 1400 feet by 1000 feet. Twin staircases of 111 steps, each 23 feet wide, led to the terrace. Great columned halls were again featured in the buildings at Persepolis. Huge porches lined with Ionic columns, some reaching 65 feet in height, flanked the halls.[3]

## Monumental Reliefs

Beginning with Cyrus the Great and continued by his successors, the Persian kings recorded the history of their reigns in giant stone reliefs. The reliefs on royal buildings and on mountainsides featured both carved figures and inscriptions that described the important events of the king's reign. Many times, the figures of the king with his followers and servants and, at time, lines of prisoners, were life-size. Many of the conquered peoples can be seen in their local dress honoring the king and bearing witness to the diversity of the empire's people. The inscription on the tomb of Darius I asks the viewer to look at the reliefs showing his throne and weapon bearers to figure out the number of countries he conquered.[4] Animals including horses, camels, and zebras are also carved on the reliefs. These reliefs were the

This griffin, a strange mythological creature, had the head and wings of an eagle and body of a lion. It is part of the artwork at palace at Persepolis.

The front side of this gold coin shows the image of Darius the Great dressed in a long tunic. He kneels, holding a drawn bow in his left hand and a long spear in his right.

testaments of the Persian kings, intended to glorify them and the empire.

## Metalwork

The other major forms of art from the Achaemenid period are works of gold and silver in the form of coins and jewelry. These coins of gold and silver bore the image of the king on bent knee with a bow and arrow.[5] They were not only valuable as money but also spread the image of the king throughout the empire.

The Persians wore gold and silver bracelets, earrings, pins, belt buckles, and belts. Persian art, whether in the form of jewelry or the reliefs that bore the images and words of the kings, was the work of artisans and artists from all over the Persian Empire, particularly the Greeks and the Egyptians. But artists from all the conquered countries contributed their artistic gifts to Persian art.[6]

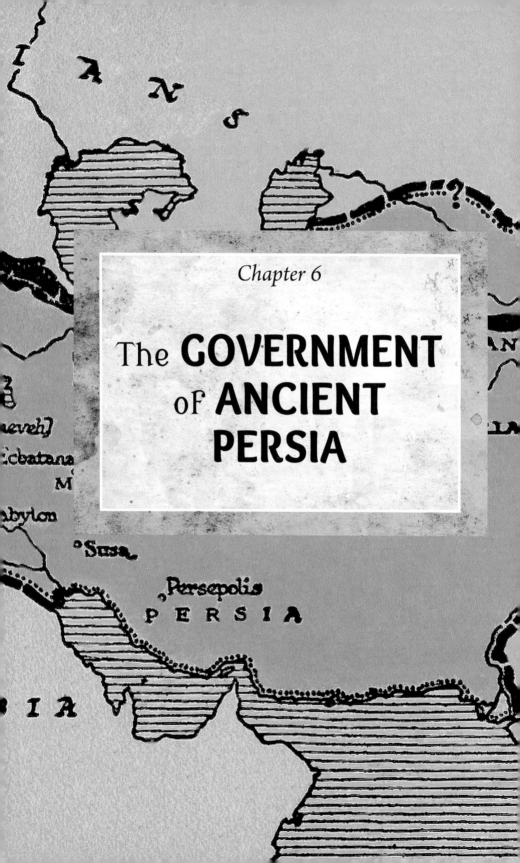

Chapter 6

# The GOVERNMENT of ANCIENT PERSIA

Under Achaemenid rule, there was no constitution or any body of law in the Persian Empire that limited the power of the king. The only limits to the king's power came from rebellion or from his own conscience. Darius I and Xerxes employed identical inscriptions to describe how they used their power to be just and protect the weak through the power that Ahura Mazda, their god, had given them.[1]

## The System of Satrapies

Darius I expanded upon a system begun by Cyrus the Great and divided his huge empire into twenty satrapies, governed by satraps.[2] Persis, as the homeland of the Persians, was not named a satrapy.

The satraps, appointed by the king, normally were members of the royal family or of Persian nobility, and they held office indefinitely. The satrap, or governor, of the

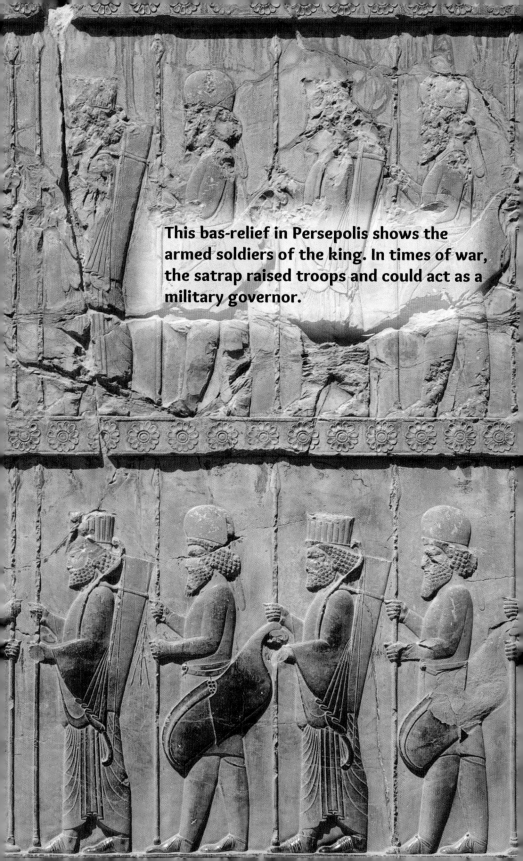

This bas-relief in Persepolis shows the armed soldiers of the king. In times of war, the satrap raised troops and could act as a military governor.

satrapies was always a Persian, but local rulers would govern under him. As long as their taxes were paid and Persian rule was accepted, each satrapy was permitted to follow local laws and traditions.[3]

The satraps carried out the civil administration of the local government such as the collection of taxes, keeping the roads safe for travel, putting down bandits and rebels, and enforcement of the peace. The satraps were also the supreme judges of the province before whom every civil and criminal case could be brought. But in times of war, the satrap raised troops and could also act as a military commander.[4]

The Persian king appointed the satraps and could remove them from power on the advice of royal clerks at the satrap's court, who functioned more or less as a secret service. The royal clerk was appointed by the king and was responsible only to the king. It was the clerk's responsibility to report to the king on the activities of the satrap.[5]

Mail carriers in the Persian Empire used a relay system that may have became the model for the Pony Express (right). Rest stops, like this caravansary, were placed at intervals along the road.

## Communication

The vast empire was held together by a 1,500-mile highway constructed and maintained by the royal government.[6] Officials guided travelers on the roads as well as reporting on what the traveler was doing. Express riders and runners used the road to bring messages to and from the various regions of the empire. At intervals along the road were inns and fortresses with fresh supplies of men and horses.[7] In this, the Persian Empire was the first to have a postal system, which functioned much like the Pony Express system of the nineteenth-century United States. The U.S. Postal Service adapted the original motto of the Persians: "Stopped by neither snow, rain, heat, or gloom of night." Communication from the satrapies to the royal government was assisted by the use of messages flashed by fire and mirrors.

Pulled by four horses, this chariot contains two figures in Median dress, linking the piece with the Achaemenid empire. The Egyptian dwarf-god, Bes, sits at the front of the chariot, which is strikingly similar to King Darius's chariot depicted on the cylinder seal.

# The Government of Ancient Persia

One of the main functions of Persepolis was to serve as the host of the ancient Zoroastrian festival, Norouz. Therefore, every year representatives from each country under the rule of Persia would bring gifts to Persepolis to show their loyalty to the king and the empire.

## The Kings' Revenue

The Persian kings acquired a great deal of their wealth through conquest, but the kings' revenue was also supplemented by taxes. Generally, each satrapy paid a fixed amount of taxes in silver.[8] In addition, a portion of the  taxes were paid through the taxation of local products and were used to feed government workers and troops.[9] Darius I imposed a tax on goods moved through canals in Babylonia.

Gifts were another important source of the Persian kings' wealth. The gifts could be precious materials such as gold and silver, but they also included presents of cattle, sheep, fruit, and wine. As the king and his court made regular travels throughout the empire, they were fed and housed by the local people, who considered this their gift to the king. Such gifts could amount to a huge expense, however, as the king traveled with an extremely large number of people, excluding portions of his army.

The Achaemenid kings produced for the first time in history a vast empire of widely differing cultures that were united under one ruler. The Persian Empire, under Achaemenid rule, gave birth to the idea of multiculturalism: a vast number of people from different backgrounds, living together in peace, with secure borders, under one ruler, and free to trade and exchange ideas and cultures with one another.[10]

# TIMELINE

**c. 3000 B.C.** Elamites are first to settle lands of ancient Persia.

**c. 1500 B.C.** Medes and Persians, nomadic tribes, move into Persia.

**c. 700 B.C.** Medes create first state in Persian plateau.

**c.550 B.C.** Achaemenid Empire: Persians under Cyrus the Great overthrow the Medes.

**c. 545 B.C.** Cyrus extends the Persian Empire by seizing Lydia and gradually gains Greek colonies in Ionia.

**539 B.C.** Cyrus captures Babylon and frees Jews in captivity there.

**529 B.C.** Cyrus dies and is succeeded by his son, Cambyses; Egypt becomes part of the Persian Empire.

**522 B.C.** Darius I becomes king of Persian Empire and reorganizes the government in system of satrapies.

**500 B.C.–449 B.C.** Persian Wars between Persian Empire and Greek city-states.

**479 B.C.–331 B.C.** Persian Empire declines.

**331 B.C.** Alexander the Great defeats a large Persian Army at Battle of Gaugamela, bringing an end to the Achaemenid Empire.

**c.313 B.C.–250 B.C.** Seleucid dynasty rules Persia following death of Alexander; Greek culture spreads throughout western and central Asia.

**250 B.C.–A.D. 224** Parthian Empire controls Persia.

**224-mid-600s** Sassanid dynasty rules Persia until the rise of Islam.

# GLOSSARY

**A.D.**—An abbreviation for the Latin anno Domini, meaning "in the year of our Lord." Used for a measurement of time, A.D. indicates the number of years since the supposed birth date of Christ.

**artisan**—A person who earns a living at a craft

**B.C.**—Before Christ. Used for a measurement of time, B.C. indicates the number of years before the supposed birth date of Christ.

**bas-relief**—a form of sculpture in which the carved figures are but partly raised from the surface of the stone

**city-state**—A city that is like an independent country.

**culture**—A people's way of life

**cuneiform**—A kind of writing used in Sumer done by making wedge-shaped marks on clay tablets.

# Glossary

**dynasty**—A series of rulers who belong to the same family.

**empire**—A nation and the country it rules.

**irrigation**—A method of bringing water to a field

**magi**—Learned men who sometimes acted as priests.

**nation**—A country with its own government.

**pharaoh**—An ancient Egyptian ruler.

**prophet**—A person who was believed to a message from God.

**satrap**—The governor of a province in ancient Persia

**satrapy**—The territory or jurisdiction of a satrap

**tribe**—A social group held together by family ties, geography, or custom.

# CHAPTER NOTES

## Chapter 1. THE EMPIRE OF CYRUS THE GREAT

1. Inscription, the Cyrus Cylinder, Yale University Library, "Ancient Seals From the Babylonian Collection," n.d., <http://www.library.yale.edu/ judaica/exhibits/webarch/front/Babylonian Collection.html#cylinderoe> (February 2, 2004).

## Chapter 2. THE LAND AND EARLY HISTORY OF ANCIENT PERSIA

1. J.M. Cook, The Persians (London: The Orion Publishing Group Ltd., 1989), p. 106.

2. Amélie Kuhrt, The Ancient Near East, Volume Two (London-New York: Routledge, 1998), p. 652.

3. Ibid., p. 545.

4. Josef Wiesehöfer, translated by Azizeh Azodi, Ancient Persia from 550 B.C. to 650 A.D. (London-New York: I.B. Tauris & Co., Ltd., 2001), pp. 44–45.

5. J.M. Cook, The Persians (London: The Orion Publishing Group Ltd., 1989), pp. 10–11.

6. Kuhrt, p. 658.

7. Cook, p. 54.

8. Ibid., p. 55.

9. Kuhrt, p. 662.

10. Ibid., p. 664.

11. Cook, p. 100.

12. Michael Grant, The Classical Greeks (United States: Book-of-the-Month Club, Inc., 1997), p. 6.

13. John Haywood, with Charles Freeman, Paul Garwood, and Judith Toms, Historical Atlas of the Classical World 500 B.C.–A.D. 600 (Cordoba, Spain: Barnes & Noble Books, 2002), p. 207.

14. Kuhrt, p. 671.

15. Ibid., p. 673.

## Chapter 3: THE RISE OF THE HELLENIC LEAGUE

1. Peter Green, Alexander of Macedon, 356–323 B.C. (Berkeley and Los Angeles: University of California Press, 1991), p. 94.

2. J.M. Cook, The Persians (London: The Orion Publishing Group Ltd., 1989), p. 338.

3. Green, pp. 179–180.

4. Cook, p. 341.

5. Chester G. Starr, A History of the Ancient World (New York: Oxford University Press, 1991), p. 398.

6. Cook, p. 342.

7. Green, pp. 319–320.

8. Cook, p. 343.

9. Green, p. 355.

## Chapter 4. LANGUAGE, RELIGION, AND PEOPLE

1. Josef Wiesehöfer, translated by Azizeh Azodi, Ancient Persia from 550 B.C. to 650 A.D. (London-New York: I.B. Tauris & Co., Ltd., 2001), p. 57.
2. Ibid., p. 44.
3. Amélie Kuhrt, The Ancient Near East, Volume Two (London-New York: Routledge, 1998), p. 663.
4. J.M. Cook, The Persians (London: The Orion Publishing Group Ltd., 1989), p. 228.
5. Ibid., p. 232.
6. Wiesehöfer, p. 95.
7. Sandra Mackey, The Iranians, Persia, Islam and the Soul of a Nation (New York: The Penguin Group, 1996), pp. 16–17.
8. Wiesehöfer, p. 36.
9. Sandra Mackey, The Iranians, Persia, Islam and the Soul of a Nation (New York: The Penguin Group, 1996), pp. 16–17.
10. Wiesehöfer, p. 69.
11. Cook, pp. 129–130.
12. Kuhrt, p. 683.

## Chapter 5. ARTS AND CULTURAL CONTRIBUTIONS

1. Sandra Mackey, The Iranians, Persia, Islam and the Soul of a Nation (New York: The Penguin Group, 1996), p. 29.

2. Amélie Kuhrt, The Ancient Near East, Volume Two (London-New York: Routledge, 1998), p. 661.
3. J.M. Cook, The Persians (London: The Orion Publishing Group Ltd., 1989), pp. 236–238.
4. Kuhrt, p. 677.
5. Cook, p. 103.
6. Ibid., p. 247.

## Chapter 6. THE GOVERNMENT OF ANCIENT PERSIA

1. Amélie Kuhrt, The Ancient Near East, Volume Two (London-New York: Routledge, 1998), p. 689.
2. J.M. Cook, The Persians (London: The Orion Publishing Group Ltd., 1989), p. 116.
3. Kuhrt, pp. 689–690.
4. Cook, p. 126.
5. Ibid., p. 126.
6. Richard F. Nyrop, ed., Iran: A Country Study (Washington, D.C.: The American University, 1978), p. 25.
7. Josef Wiesehöfer, translated by Azizeh Azodi, Ancient Persia from 550 B.C. to 650 A.D. (London-New York: I.B. Tauris & Co., Ltd., 2001), p. 77.
8. Cook, p. 303.
9. Wiesehöfer, p. 67.
10. Cook, p. 344.

# FURTHER READING

## BOOKS

Burgan, Michael. *Empires of Ancient Persia.* New York: Chelsea House Publishers, 2009.

Cheshire, Gerard, and Paula Hammond. *The Middle East.* Broomall, Pa.: Mason Crest Publishers, 2003.

Crompton, Samuel Willard. *Alexander the Great.* Philadelphia: Chelsea House Publishers, 2003.

———. *Cyrus the Great.* New York: Chelsea House Publishers, 2008.

Nardo, Don. *Ancient Persia.* San Diego, Calif.: Blackbirch Press, 2004.

Poolos, J. *Darius the Great.* New York: Chelsea House Publishers, 2008.

Schecter, Vicky Alvear. *Alexander the Great Rocks the World.* Plain City, OH: Darby Creek Pub., 2006.

Schomp, Virginia. *The Ancient Persians.* New York: Marshall Cavendish Benchmark, 2010.

Spencer, Lauren. *Iran: A Primary Source Cultural Guide.* New York: Rosen Publishing Group, 2003.

Woods, Michael. *Seven Wonders of the Ancient Middle East.* Minneapolis, MN: Twenty-First Century Books, 2008.

## INTERNET ADDRESSES

**Factmonster: Persia—An Introduction**
<http://www.factmonster.com/encyclopedia/
history/persia.html>

**The Metropolitan Museum of Art: Heilbrunn
Timeline of Art History—The Achaemenid
Persian Empire (550–330 B.C.)**
<http://www.metmuseum.org/toah/hd/acha/
hd_acha.htm>

# INDEX

## A

Achaemenes, 23
Achaemenid Empire, rulers of
   Artaxerxes I, 38, 76
   Artaxerxes II, 38-39
   Cambyses II, 11, 25-28,57
   Cyrus II, Cyrus the Great,
     8-15, 23-25, 31, 38, 57,
     63, 74-77, 83
   Darius I, 12, 17-23, 28-29,
     46, 63-66, 74, 76-77, 83,
     92
   Darius II, 20, 38
   Darius III, 39, 41-47
   Xerxes, 34-38, 46, 76, 83
   Xerxes II, 38
Afghanistan, 17, 20, 50
Alexander the Great, 10,
   41-47
arts, 74-81
Artystone, 63
Aryans, 8-10
Assyrian Empire, 11, 20, 74
Astyages, 10

## B

Babylonia, 11, 15, 20, 24-25,
   34, 54-55, 92
Behistun Inscription, 29
Bessos, 46-47
Bulgaria, 17
Byzantine Empire, 52

## C

Constantinople, 52
Croesus, 23
Cyrus Cylinder, 15, 23, 55

## D

daily life, 62-72
Dardanelles, 29, 37, 41

## E

Egypt, 11, 17-28, 34, 39, 43,
   47
Elamites, 8
Ephesus, 42

## F

Fars, 17, 20

# Index

## G
Gaugamela, battle of, 46
geography, 17-20
government, 8, 62-63, 83-93
Granicus, battle of, 42
Greek city-states
    Athens, 24, 31, 37-38, 46
    Eretria, 24
    Sparta, 37-38

## H
Hellenic League, 41

## I
India, 29, 69
Ionia, 11, 24, 31, 39, 69
Iran, 8-10, 17, 20, 76
Iraq, 11, 17
Islam, 52
Issus, battle of, 43

## J
Jerusalem, 31, 55

## L
languages, 12, 24, 29, 54-55
Leonidas, 37
Lydia, 11, 23-24

## M
Macedonia, 31, 41-43
Medes, Median Empire, 8-10, 20-23
Mithridates, 42

## P
Pakistan, 17, 25, 31

Parthian Empire, 50-52
Pasargadae, 74
Persepolis, 34, 46, 63, 74, 76
Persian Wars,
    Battle of Marathon, 31, 34
    Battle of Thermopylae, 37
    Battles of Salamis and Plataea, 37
Persis, 8, 17, 83
Philip I of Macedonia, 41-42
Ptolemy I, 47

## S
Sardis, 23, 42, 69
Sassanid dynasty, 50-52
satrapies, 25, 31, 83-88
Seleucid dynasty, 47
Susa, 34, 43, 46, 66-69, 74
Syria, 17, 43, 46

## T
Teispes, 20-23
Thrace, 17, 29-31
Tigris River, 11, 46
Turkey, 11, 17
Tyre, 43

## X
Xenophon, 54

## Z
Zagros Mountains, 17, 24
Zoroaster, 57, 58
Zoroastrianism, 57, 62